C000220187

IMAGES OF *Hinckley* and District

The Hinckley Times

IMAGES OF Hinckley and District

The Breedon Books
Publishing Company
Derby

First published in Great Britain by
The Breedon Books Publishing Company Limited
Breedon House, 44 Friar Gate, Derby, DE1 1DA.
1996

Acknowledgements

The publishers gratefully acknowledge the following people who helped to compile *Images of Hinckley*. Mr F.W.Bones, Mrs M.Orton, Mrs J.Philps, Mr S.J.Tomlinson, Mr T.Wheatley, Mrs G.Wood, Mr G.Wright.

ISBN 1 85983 054 4

Printed and bound by Butler & Tanner Ltd., Selwood Printing Works, Caxton Road, Frome, Somerset.

Colour separations by Colour Services, Wigston, Leicester.

Jackets printed by Lawrence-Allen, Weston-super-Mare, Avon

Contents

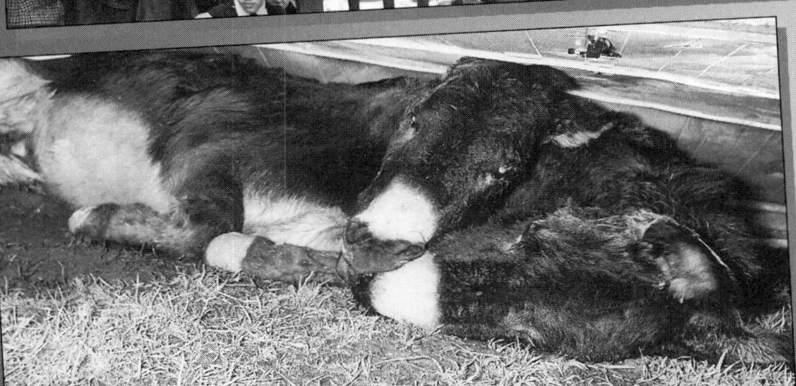

Foreword

A LOCAL newspaper holds a uniquely privileged position in the local community. With the trust, affection and respect of its readers it fulfils many important functions. It informs them, entertains them, gives them a platform for their views, acts as a watchdog on their behalf and often becomes a close friend.

And one other thing it does extraordinarily well is to record, in words and pictures, the everyday lives of the people who live in the community, and the changing face of their environment.

The Hinckley Times has been doing this for over 106 years. A glance through the back issues of the newspaper reveals images of the shifting fashions, trends and lifestyles of the townspeople, as well as the changing architecture of the town as it has developed this century.

This book is a dip into the images of decades past. In many ways it can only scratch the surface of the history it attempts to record, but we hope the careful selection of photographs will provide a flavour of the town's past and that of the surrounding area.

David Potter
Editor
The Hinckley Times

Before World War One

The Atherstone Hunt gather at the Three Pots, Burbage, in November 1908.

The Burbage Military Orchestra and Band, probably pictured around 1910.

Crowds gather for the marriage of Mr H.P.Atkins to Miss Dorothy Moore at Burbage Church on 23 June 1909.

Church Street, Burbage, pictured in 1918.

The Anchor Inn, Burbage (centre of picture) and John Carrigan's tobacconist business (right). The sign over his shop reads: 'London and North-Western Railway Parcels Received and Forwarded To All Parts.' Another reads: 'Lucky Star Cigarettes 6 for 1d.' The photograph was taken in 1906.

Burbage Church photographed in 1916.

Woodman's Cottage, Burbage Woods, probably in 1910.

Windsor End (now Windsor Street), Burbage, in 1911. Freeman's Lane is off to the right.

Three residents of Horsepool House, Burbage, pictured at the front gate around 1909.

All dressed up for the 'Olde English Market Fayre' at Burbage on 17 September 1910.

A review of the Church Lads' Brigade at Sketchley on Whit Monday, 1907.

The Horsepool, Burbage, in 1904. The picture is from a postcard addressed to Taunton in Somerset and on the reverse is a message: 'Thanks for the mistletoe.'

The High Street at Barwell in 1911.

These fine gentlemen are members of the Barwell Brass Band and were pictured around 1911.

The Barwell Coronation Committee pictured at the old people's tea they had organised in the village school playground on 22 June 1911.

The Atherstone Hunt meets at Barwell on 27 December 1912.

The May Queen and her attendants at the Barwell Children's Summer Festival around 1904.

Rows of terraced houses in Queen Street, Barwell, in 1908.

Chapel Street, Barwell, in 1906, looking towards Top Town. In the background a man and a young girl get water from a street pump.

Ministers in procession to a dedication service at Barwell Parish Church on 29 June 1905.

The Three Crowns at Barwell and a row of terraced houses named Co-operative Terrace and built in 1884.

Barwell Parish Church choir pictured outside the church in 1905.

The interior of Barwell Parish Church pictured around 1912.

The bridge across the Soar at Croft in 1906. The Heathcote Arms, then an Everard's pub, overlooks the scene.

The new village hall at Croft in 1906.

Croft Church and Rectory in 1906.

Dancing girls at Croft Fête, 9 July 1904.

The Parsons & Sherwin Co Ltd stand at Leicestershire Agricultural Show in July 1909. Their stand was awarded the silver medal. Notices on the stand inform of the opening of their new showroom on Station Road, Hinckley. It was an old-established business that is no more.

Pupils and teachers gather for a photograph at Market Bosworth Grammar School in 1903. The school is now known as the Dixie Grammar School.

Market Bosworth Grammar School has altered little since this photograph was taken in 1902. Only the name has changed, to the Dixie Grammar School.

The Rectory, Market Bosworth, in 1904.

The Old Black Horse Inn, Market Bosworth, in 1904. The landlord at that time was Joseph Palmer Esq.

A proud mother and her baby on the doorstep of a house in Park Street, Market Bosworth, in 1904. Is that the equally proud father a few yards down the street?

The Market Place at Market Bosworth in 1904.

The Atherstone Hunt meets in the Market Place at Market Bosworth in March 1914.

The hounds make their appearance at Market Bosworth Grammar School as the Atherstone Hunt meet there in March 1914.

The interior of Market Bosworth Church, pictured in 1905.

This 'Henry' who reigned at Bosworth Field in 1916 had a crown of grey hair and gave a hearty welcome to visitors.

We now know it as the A444 but when this photograph was taken in 1910 it was simply the quiet main road through Twycross. The building on the left is the Post Office.

The main road through Twycross again, this time with the Curzon Arms on the left. The landlord in 1910 was Mr W.Peach.

Twycross House in 1910. It is now the home of Twycross House School.

This photograph, taken in 1905, shows the interior of Peckleton Church.

No transport of any kind in sight in Wolvey Village in 1905.

Another tranquil scene from Wolvey Village, this time looking towards the church in 1910.

Three children pose in the main street of Peckleton Village pictured in 1905.

Kirkby Mallory villagers gather for a photograph in 1908.

Village life in Kirkby Mallory in the golden days before World War One.

The splendid Hall at Kirkby Mallory, sadly no longer in existence.

"Bless you my children," says the Emperor to the Prince and Princess in this Hinckley High School production of the Princess Ju Ju operetta staged in April 1904.

High Street, Earl Shilton, pictured around 1908. A wagon, minus its horse, is parked outside the King William IV public house. Opposite is the Colonial Meat Co with a butcher at the doorway. Front right is the Midland Drapery Co.

The Earl Shilton cricket team which met Barwell in June 1904.

Earl Shilton School cricket team, winners of the 1904 Challenge Shield.

Wood Street, Earl Shilton, in about 1907, looking very different to that of today. Everyone was confident enough to pose for the camera while standing in the middle of the road.

Thurlaston Village in 1906. Again, the camera has attracted the attention of some local residents.

Normanton Hall, Thurlaston, in 1910.

A little girl sits on the steps of a shop at Stoke Golding in 1917. The shop is advertising White Rose American Lamp Oil. Further down the street an apparently camera-shy lady looks the other way.

The George and Dragon at Stoke Golding in 1907. The landlord at that time was Mr K.Geary.

Children pose beside a horse-drawn threshing machine at Sharnford Village in 1904.

The vicar of Sharnford pictured outside the Rectory with his children, one on horseback the other astride a donkey, in 1909.

The main thoroughfare, now designated the B4114, cuts through Sharnford Village much as it does today. The Blue Bell Inn and the Old Star Inn are opposite each other.

The result of a landslide at Stoney Stanton on 18 December 1910.

The Stoney Stanton Rising Star football team pictured before a Hinckley Hospital Charity Cup match in 1905.

Scholars and staff at Stoney Stanton School line up for the camera in 1910.

Higham-on-the-Hill as it looked in 1905. On the left is the Barley Sheaf Inn, landlord George Dutton.

The Oddfellows Arms, Higham-on-the-Hill, in 1905.

This gentleman poses near the water pump at Higham-on-the-Hill in 1905. He guards two bicycles, one of them presumably belonging to the photographer.

The infant children of Higham-on-the-Hill School in 1906.

These gentlemen are taking part in the centenary celebrations of the Independent Order of Oddfellows at Hinckley in September 1910.

Hinckley Parish Church choristers pictured at Christmas 1916.

The Hinckley Town Band in March 1907.

The Hinckley Sunday School Union Treat of July 1908.

Hinckley Territorials gather at the junction of New Buildings and Wood Street to answer the call of King

and Country in August 1914.

The Hinckley Sunday School Union Festival of July 1905. On the back of the picture in a childish hand are the words: 'Puzzle. Find Me. Louisa Carter.'

All aboard for the Hinckley St Mary's Sunday School Treat in July 1907.

General Booth, founder of the Salvation Army visited Hinckley on 8 August 1905 and here crowds gather in the Market Place to hear him speak. A banner proclaims: 'God Bless You, General.'

Pupils and staff of Mrs Whatmore's High School, Hinckley, in 1903.

Laying of the foundation stone of the new Catholic Schools at Hinckley, on Easter Monday 1907.

Crowds gather for the opening of the new bandstand in Queen's Park, Hinckley, on 28 May 1908.

And this is Queen's Park, Hinckley, just after the bandstand was opened.

Peace celebrations to mark the end of World War One, held in Hinckley in July 1919, some eight months after the Armistice was signed.

Children in their best frocks and carrying flowers at the 1919 peace celebrations in Hinckley.

Flags and bunting adorn the Market Place and The Borough as Hinckley celebrates the coronation of King George V in June 1911. The United Counties Bank is on the left and in the distance can be seen the Union Hotel.

The scene from the bottom of Castle Street, Hinckley, in 1912.

St Mary's Church spire breaks the horizon. Brick Kiln Street is in the foreground. Its houses are now long gone.

Looking along Regent Street with its junction of Coventry Road and Lancaster Road crossing it, pictured 1917. The Prince's Feathers, selling Marston's Burton Ales, is on the left.

A traffic-free Highfield Road, Hinckley, in 1914.

Station Road, one view of Hinckley that does not appear to have changed that much since this photograph was taken in 1916.

Hinckley Liberal Club in the first decade of the 20th century. Next door to it stands the Royal Oak.

This 1914 view of Hill Street shows houses on the right where Hinckley's Health Centre now stands.

Factory Road, Hinckley, in 1917. People can still saunter up the middle of the road although a motor cycle is parked on the right.

Another view of Castle Street at the beginning of this century.

A splendid view of The Borough in 1902. Market stalls are in place ready for the day's business.

The Union Hotel, Hinckley, looking very much as it does today. The signs on the wall advertise a Midland Railway parcels service.

The Market Place, Hinckley, with the George Inn. The picture is around 1914. On the reverse is written: 'Thanks for your letter. By the look of the papers you'll soon all be soldiers. It's awful here at night with no lights at all.'

Derby Road, Hinckley, as it looked in 1906. A police officer and a local tradesman pose for the camera.

Left: Mr Harry Newman is about to set off with the mail before the turn of the century. His cart carries an advertisement for Northampton Races.

Below: This photograph, taken from St Mary's Church bell tower, shows St Mary's School in the foreground and Station Road, Further on is Regent Street, many of whose buildings have changed little since this photograph was taken at the turn of the century.

The stout-hearted men of Hinckley Fire Brigade before World War One. Those pictured are (back row, left to right): Messrs Throne senior, Newman and Baggott. Front are Chapman, Hood, Reid, Warner, Reynolds and Flavell.

Grims Lane, Hinckley, now known as New Buildings. The picture was taken around World War One.

Mansion Street and Lower Bond Street. The Liberal Club is to the left. This time among the people looking at

the camera is a milkman, standing at the rear of his horse-drawn cart.

The Twenties and the Thirties

Hundreds gather in Argent's Mead as Hinckley's memorial to those who perished in World War One is unveiled in May 1922.

The Earl Shilton memorial to those who died in World War One was unveiled in October 1920. Relatives of the fallen are seen laying wreaths.

On a Saturday morning in February 1921 the war memorial at Burbage was unveiled.

Crowds gather at Top Town, Barwell, on New Year's Eve 1922 for the unveiling of the war memorial there.

Children in their Sunday best walk along Leicester Road, Hinckley, in 1926.

Flags and flowers at Hinckley Sunday School Union Treat in 1929.

Queen's Road, Hinckley, in the 1920s. The scene has changed little today, save for the now ubiquitous rows of parked cars.

A tree-lined Clarendon Road, Hinckley, in the early 1920s with a postman pausing from his round to be captured by the camera.

Princess Alice (seated), other dignitaries and nurses pictured at 'Ye Olde English Fayre', which the princess has just opened at Hinckley Hospital in June 1922.

Children in their costumes at 'Ye Olde English Fayre' at Hinckley Hospital in June 1922.

Castle Street on a winter's afternoon in 1924, showing the new Gas Showrooms.

St Peter's School Treat passes through Castle Street, Hinckley, in July 1920.

Another Sunday School procession, this time that of Hinckley Sunday Schools Union Treat in July 1921.

This view taken from the Gas Works in 1929 makes Hinckley look a very industrial town.

A cyclist pedals one way, a lone motor car comes the other on Leicester Road, Hinckley, in the 1920s.

Proud schoolboys clamber aboard a World War One tank which was presented to Hinckley in February 1920

Stoke Golding war memorial shortly after it was unveiled in the village in the early 1920s.

The New Buildings, Hinckley, in 1926 with the Wesleyan Chapel on the left and Argyle House on the right.

The Grammar School, Hinckley, in the 1920s.

Men of Brass. Hinckley Salvation Army Band in 1920. There is one lady member pictured.

The Weaver's Arms is just visible to the left in this view of Derby Avenue – now just plain old Derby Road – Hinckley, in 1920.

Upper Castle Street, Hinckley, in the 1920s. The New Inn, selling Marston's Ales, is to the right.

In this 1920s view, The Borough, Hinckley, looks very peaceful.

Queen's Road, Hinckley, in the 1920s.

Is that as busy as it got? A cyclist glides down Station Road, Hinckley, in the 1920s.

Hinckley St Paul's football team pictured in the 1922-23 season.

'Waifs and Strays' pageant at the Hinckley Palladium in November 1924.

A view of Church Street, Burbage, in the 1920s.

The Salvation Army proclaimed Self-Denial Week from 3-10 March 1923. In The Borough, Hinckley, people were invited to 'turn pounds of pennies into tons of joy for thousands of people'.

Firemen in attendance at Bennett Brothers hosiery factory, Southfield Road, Hinckley, in 1928.

A party of Hinckley people prepare to board a special train at Hinckley Station to be taken to the British Empire Exhibition at Wembley in 1924.

This charabanc is about to leave Hinckley for a day trip in the early 1930s. It is outside the Hinckley Coffee House in the Market Place. A sign above reveals that this was also the meeting place for the Independent Order of Rechabites.

The picturesque Market Place, Hinckley, in 1932. This view has hardly altered from that of 1914 pictured earlier in this book.

Station Road, Hinckley, in the 1930s.

The Technical Schools, Hinckley.

The Regent Cinema, Hinckley. The film advertised is *Guilty Hands* with a Laurel and Hardy supporting feature.

Three ladies, two of them holding small children pose in Lower Coventry Road, Hinckley, in the 1930s.

This picture of Lower Coventry Road, is empty of people save for the cyclist who has paused on the left.

Lady and gentleman out for a stroll in Beaumont Avenue, Hinckley before the war.

New Buildings, Hinckley, in the 1930s.

There is a little more traffic in this scene of Regent Street, Hinckley, albeit all the cars are parked.

A tranquil pre-war scene at Argent's Mead, Hinckley.

The Wharf Inn, Hinckley, with the landlady posing in the doorway.

The Garden of Remembrance, Hinckley.

The Rock Gardens, Hinckley.

The Cottage Hospital, Hinckley, in the 1930s.

Almey's Lane, Earl Shilton.

Upper Hinckley Road, Earl Shilton.

This Hinckley football team of the 1930-31 season won three splendid silver trophies.

Hinckley RFC players and officials for the 1937-38 season.

The Post-war Era

These children are pictured at the VE Day celebrations at the Rock Gardens, Coventry Road, Hinckley, in May 1945.

Tea and cakes for these partygoers from Queen's Road and Princess Street, Hinckley, who are celebrating VJ Day in August 1945.

Burbage School leavers of 1947, classes 4A and 4B.

Hinckley Grammar School rugby team of 1947-48.

The Burbage Silver Prize Band pictured in 1948.

Coventry Road, Hinckley, looking towards Regent Street in the 1950s.

The junction of Regent Street and Coventry Road, Hinckley.

These houses on Derby Road, Hinckley, are long gone and it is now the site of the Kingdom Hall.

Rear of the houses on Victoria Street, Hinckley, pictured in the 1950s.

Joan Veasey, the Hinckley Carnival Queen for 1950, is pictured here duly crowned and with her attendants.

The 1950 Hinckley Carnival Queen, Joan Veasey, presents trophies to the football club.

A Hinckley Sunday Schools Walk in the 1950s.

Members of Westfield Church pictured at a Hinckley Sunday Schools Walk in the 1950s.

More children enjoying the Hinckley Sunday Schools Walk.

In January 1952, Harold MacMillan, then the Minister of Housing but later in the decade to become Prime Minister, visited Hinckley to formally open Bosworth Rural Council's 'Under £1,000' housing scheme at Desford. Here Mr MacMillan chats to tenants Mr and Mrs Reast at the door to one of the properties.

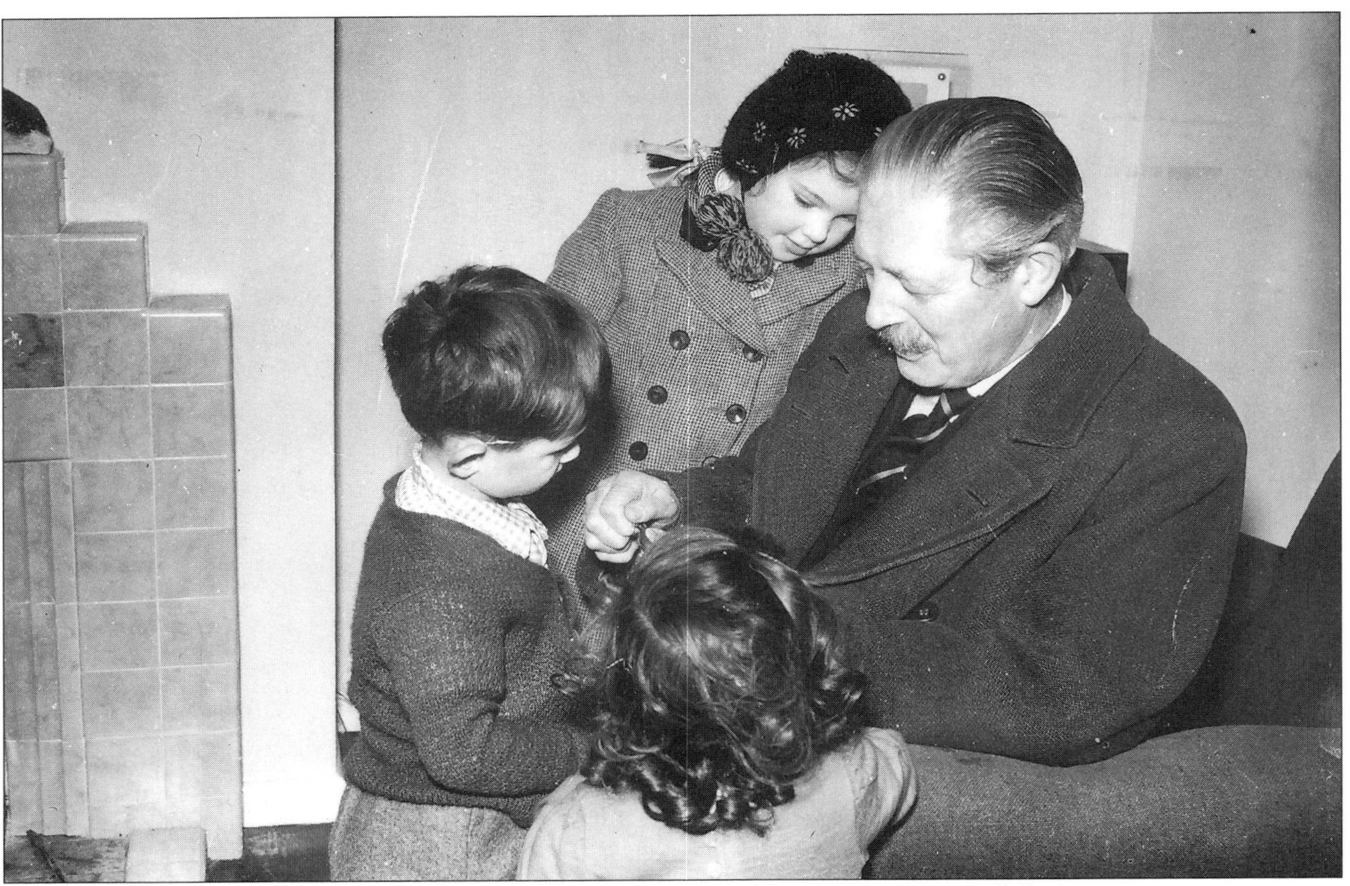

Mr MacMillan has a chat with Mr and Mrs Reast's two children and a friend of theirs.

The Minister for Housing is shown around the Reast's home.

The Sharnford Silver Band pictured in 1953.

June 1953 and a Coronation Tea at Westfield School for the residents of Coventry Road and Rosemary Way.

Workers at a Hinckley hosiery factory pictured hard at work in the 1950s.

Guests at Hinckley Rugby Club annual ball in the 1950s.

Church parade of the Sharnford Lodge of the RAOB, pictured in the grounds of the Rectory in 1954.

Hinckley Ladies Hockey Club pictured at their Coventry Road ground in 1955.

Hinckley Ladies Cricket Club at the Coventry Road ground in 1955.

Sgt Don Cobley of the RAF and Barwell, pictured in 1958. Sgt Cobley was three times British pentathlon champion and represented Great Britain in the 1956 and 1960 Olympic Games, in Melbourne and Rome respectively. In Melbourne, he ran the race of his life in the modern pentathlon cross-country event, winning it by 13 seconds.

The Sixties and Seventies

The Victoria Hotel, Upper Castle Street, Hinckley, pictured in January 1960.

The White Hart, which stood at the bottom of Castle Street, Hinckley, in March 1960. The landlord at that time was Horace Storer.

The Half Moon, pictured in March 1960 on Stockwell Head, Hinckley, when the landlord was Thomas Smith.

Buy a Rag Mag please! Rag Day at Hinckley in March 1960.

Elephants in Hinckley! The circus comes to town in April 1960.

Sapcote Methodists' Sunday School procession in May 1960.

Stanhope's butcher's flank the East Yorkshire School of Motoring in The Borough, Hinckley, in September 1960.

Mr Rex Fray, manager of the Gaumont Cinema, Hinckley, pictured in September 1960.

Champion motor cyclist Mike Hailwood gets a congratulatory kiss after winning the £1,000 Race of the Year at Mallory Park in September 1960.

Hinckley's Tin Hat went on display at the Odeon Cinema in November 1960. It was purchased in 1911 by Mr Tom Pratt for ten guineas (£10.50). The Tin Hat was made by Tinker Jenning, whose workshop was in Trinity Lane, and the Hat was reported to hold 34½ pints.

In February 1961, this was regarded as a busy Regent Street, Hinckley.

Hinckley in May 1961. On the left is the Odeon Cinema in The Borough, then Liggins sweet shop and shops in The Borough Chambers.

Dancers of Monica Mason's Sunbeams step out in April 1961.

Boys and girls are smartly turned out for speech day at Hastings High School in July 1961.

In August 1961, H.Merry's newsagency business stood in what was the Union Hotel Block, Lower Bond Street, Hinckley.

For many years these houses stood at the side of Cock Hill on the outskirts of Burbage. This picture was taken in April 1962, just before demolition began.

It took three months to demolish the Odeon Theatre and 3,000 tons of rubble and a 76ft-long girder were just part of the problem. This photograph was taken in August 1962 and the Nationwide Building Society now stands on this site in The Borough, Hinckley, although the building which replaced the Odeon initially housed the Leicestershire Building Society.

May 1963 and this was the scene at the 102nd annual May fair at Market Bosworth. Cattle market auctioneer Mr Tom Hackney was taking bids then, as he was in 1996 when the Cattle Market closed its doors for the last time.

In the summer of 1963 heavy rains made gathering in the corn harvest look a well-nigh impossibility, but an 'Indian Summer' helped to ensure that the harvest was in before winter set in. This photograph on the outskirts of Hinckley was taken in September that year.

A huge convoy thunders down Castle Street, Hinckley, in the days before pedestrianisation. This 'road train

neasured 198ft from end to end and contained 96 wheels.

In April 1964, Stoney Stanton's Easter Monday Pram Race was one of the leading local attractions. Councillor George Marriott (standing) was a regular participant and can be seen here with Mr R.D.Holton. The Pram Race may be a thing of the past but Councillor Marriott can still be seen bringing a smile to Stoney Stanton Carnival.

This doesn't look much like a motor cycle sidecar, but that is exactly what it was raced as. In February 1965 controversy raged as Owen Greenwood raced his machine to some considerable success. Well, it did comply to the regulations then prevailing.

In January 1965, two of British soccer's most well-known faces – Tommy Docherty, then the manager of Chelsea, and Terry Venables, the Chelsea skipper, an England international and future manager– visited the Hinckley area to sign a contract with Barwell boot and shoe firm, Geo Ward Ltd. Here, Tommy Docherty examines the new boot at Wightman's Sports with Mr Reg Wightman.

Terry Venables signs the contract, watched by the chairman of the Geo Ward Group, Mr W.J.Jobson.

Hinckley RFC pictured during the 1964-65 season, when they managed to go right through the campaign without being beaten on their home ground.

In March 1965, Norman Dagley of Earl Shilton became the All-England Amateur Billiards champion and later in his career went on to lift the world title.

Watery Gate, Earl Shilton, had a nasty habit of flooding and catching out the occasional motorist, as here in March 1965.

A view of Regent Street, Hinckley, taken in May 1965. It is a scene that has changed little over the years, apart from the shop names, and is instantly recognisable 30 years later.

In June 1965, motor racing champion Graham Hill thrilled Bank Holiday crowds at the Mallory Park circuit. Hill later met a tragic end but 30 years later his son, Damon, was a world-famous name in the sport.

In September 1965, Hinckley's Monday market was as familiar a part of the town's life as it is today. One thing has changed, however. You'll no longer hear any stallholder shouting, "Five oranges for a shilling!"

We wouldn't like to say if he was the most unpopular man in Hinckley in November 1965. Probably not. But Mr D.Jones did become the town's first traffic warden that month.

December 1965 and Jacques in Castle Street have lit up their shop as Christmas approaches.

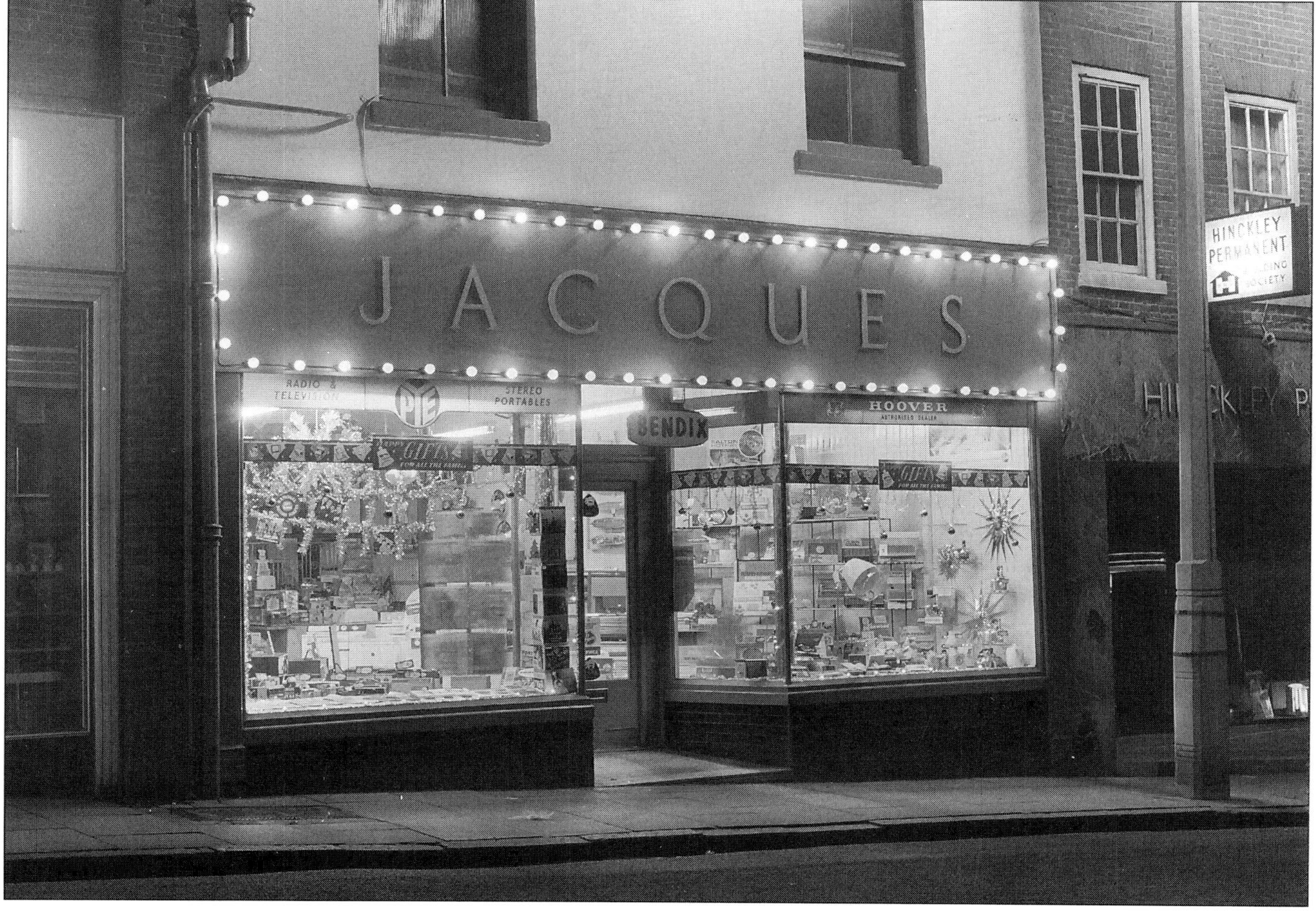

Hinckley's Christmas lights again, this time at the Co-op in Castle Street.

Members of Hinckley Baptist Church present their Nativity Play in December 1965.

A heavenly portent? On Christmas Eve 1965 a meteor fell in Barwell, part of it coming through the window of Mr and Mrs Grewcock.

This was the scene at the bottom of Castle Street, Hinckley, in January 1966 after a fire had damaged the premises of J.J.Edwards, the travel and shipping company, and Tattersall's grocer's shop.

Regent Street, Hinckley, in August 1967. A few children are strolling, making the most of the last few days of the long summer holiday.

In April 1968 a fleet of 'panda cars' began patrolling the streets of Hinckley. Here the officers line up beside their vehicles, ready for the off.

In July 1968 the heaviest rain the Hinckley area had seen for many years flooded the main road through Sharnford.

Lord Fisher, a former Archbishop of Canterbury and the son of a Higham-on-the-Hill rector, officially opened the new Hinckley Council offices in July 1968.

In September 1968 Freddie Garraty of the pop group Freddie and the Dreamers opened the new Tesco supermarket in Castle Street, Hinckley. Jacques shop opposite seems to have done quite well for publicity too!

In October 1968 Burbage started cooking on North Sea gas. Here the last of the old 'town gas' is burned off in Winchester Drive. Conversion to natural gas was an enormous operation and contemporary reports likened Burbage to 'a village under invasion'.

In February 1969, shortly before his retirement as superintendent at Hinckley Public Baths, Ted Ellis who had taught thousands of Hinckley youngsters to swim, got the surprise of his life when a BBC TV crew turned up to film him for *Midlands Today*. Some years later Mr Ellis opened Hinckley's Leisure Centre and was later awarded the MBE.

On 7 February 1969 Hinckley came to a standstill, traffic was going nowhere and all roads were blocked. Journeys from Leicester and Coventry were taking eight hours as the whole of the Midlands ground to a halt under a blanket of snow.

In April 1969 Sir Wolstan Dixie-Bart put the market back into Market Bosworth. It had been over 50 years since a market had been held in the town but Sir Wolstan claimed that he was entitled to hold one under a charter granted to one of his ancestors by Charles II.

Happy faces at Stoke Golding Church of England School in April 1969 when the PTA presented the school with a new climbing frame.

In November 1969 Mr Edward Heath, leader of the Conservative Party, opened the £30,000 extension to Barwell Constitutional Club.

November 1969 still; traffic flow problems in Barwell were to lead to the removal of the war memorial which had been unveiled 47 years earlier.

In February 1970, the Barwell war memorial had disappeared from Top Town. It was erected on New Year's Eve 1922.

Regent Street, Hinckley, in November 1969 showing the newly-erected Christmas lights.

In February 1970 the Rotary movement celebrated its 65th anniversary. This is Hinckley Rotary Club. Back row (left to right): Rotarians A.B.Mills, J.W.Gilbert, F.E.Downes, J.E.Francis, H.Young, G.Walmsley, A.Payne, C.B.Cotton, V.Forster and Dr F.C.Johnson. Third row: Rotarians H.M.Etherington, S.J.Thompson, D.J.Dawson, M.J.Whitmore, S.F.Powell, R.F.A.Smallshaw, A.K.Davey, past president E.J.L.Cotton and R.T.Stevens. Second row: Past presidents H.Stones, A.B.Coley, J.E.Payne, F.Boulter, C.L.Payne, J.O.Prytherch, F.Taylor, J.Pickering, F.Oldham, J.S.Randle, G.N.Anderson and F.C.Dudley. Front row: Rotarians W.H.Smallbone, H.R.Lockley, A.Edwards, E.Davison, president Revd E.W.Platt, W.O.Ruffle, J.V.Allen, R.E.Bennett, past president J.T.L.Baxter and A.S.Russell.

In the General Election of June 1970, a countryside swing to the Conservatives changed many safe Labour seats into Tory victories. Mr Adam Butler would now represent the Bosworth constituency in Parliament. Mr Woodrow Wyatt was the outgoing MP. It was the first time that Bosworth had gone to the Conservatives since 1924. Here Mr Butler is seen with his wife, Felicity, celebrating victory in the Market Place, Hinckley.

In April 1970 traffic in Hinckley was diverted as a huge crane was employed to deliver a computer to Barclay's Bank in the Market Place. Today, a computer with the same memory capacity could be carried through the front door in someone's pocket.

Comedy legend Norman Wisdom lends a hand at Hinckley's new theatre, The Concordia, in April 1972.

On 26 May 1972, HRH Princess Margaret, Countess of Snowden, opened a new extension to the Hinckley factory of Messrs Atkins Ltd. Here the princess is accompanied by Mr Daniel Styles, chairman and managing director of the company.

Atkins workers applaud Princess Margaret during her tour of the factory.

The Billiard Hall on Station Road, Hinckley, pictured in September 1972. It was demolished months later.

In May 1973, J.Robinson & Sons of Burbage celebrated 50 years 'on the buses'.

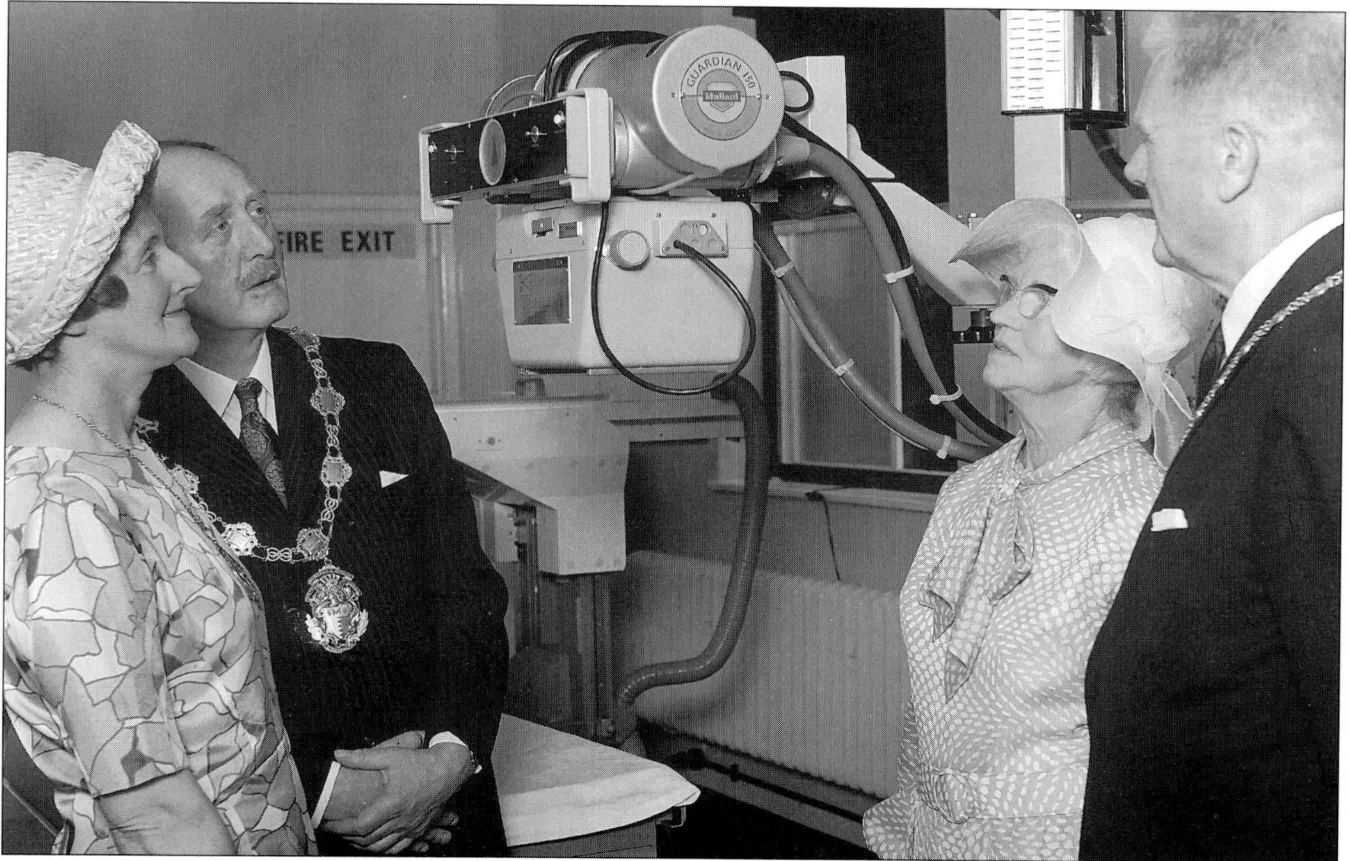

Hinckley's new X-ray unit is opened in June 1973. It took four years of hard work by the public of Hinckley to raise the money for the new unit.

Hinckley's Sunday Schools gather in Atkins' car park for a short service in July 1973, following the Procession

of Christian Witnesses.

The corner of Trinity Lane and Coventry Road, Hinckley, in July 1973, before the bulldozers moved in.

Some 133 years after it was built, Trinity Hall is demolished to make way for Hinckley's new sports centre.

Just an ordinary scene of workers at a Hinckley hosiery factory? Well, not quite. Under the Electricity Economy Regulations prevailing during industrial action in January 1974, shops and offices were allowed to use electricity only at pre-determined times.

The bottom of Castle Street, Hinckley, in March 1974 as the area was prepared for the erection of new offices for the Hinckley and Country Building Society, later to become the Town and Country Building Society.

March 1974: We got it! The time by Big Ben is 11.30am with the Palace of Westminster and the River Thames in the background. Councillor Ted Brown, chairman of the new district council, holds the Royal Charter which gave Hinckley its borough status and made Councillor Brown the town's first mayor.

November 1974 and Britannia Yard is demolished to make way for a new shopping centre – the Britannia Centre.

Whenever word got out in December 1974 that a particular shop had bread for sale, queues would surely form. The scene was the same across the country during a nationwide dispute among bakery workers. This queue, reminiscent of wartime when shortages meant long lines outside almost every shop, are waiting patiently in Castle Street, Hinckley.

In February 1975, Hinckley shoppers were treated to a new view from Castle Street, a view taking in Stockwell Head and Council Road with the Concordia Theatre just visible to the right. Developers demolishing the former premises of Larkes, Matkins & Hiltons had opened up a sight which would soon disappear again as the Britannia Centre was completed.

Firemen are tackling the £300,000 blaze at the Sketchley Overall Department in Hinckley in August 1975.

On the Sunday afternoon of 21 February 1975, a carelessly discarded cigarette caused a £50,000 blaze at the Regent Club. This view shows the main corridor, where the fire was believed to have started. The wooden battens, from which the panelling was stripped by the blaze, are visible. A parade of shops now stands on the site.

September 1975: pedestrianisation, a good idea or not? One shopper described the three-month trial scheme in Hinckley as 'a bit pathetic', adding that 'people daren't walk on the road in case one of the delivery vans runs them over'. Twenty-one years later, Castle Street remains pedestrianised.

Trouble at tip as council workman strike in November 1975. Market stalls in Hinckley were left standing and rubbish was not collected as 150 council manual workers withdrew their labour for two days. Their senior shop steward, Mr Fred Knight of Holt Road, Burbage, said that the strike was called in protest at the instant dismissal of a worker at the Barwell tip after he had salvaged an article from rubbish which had been dumped there.

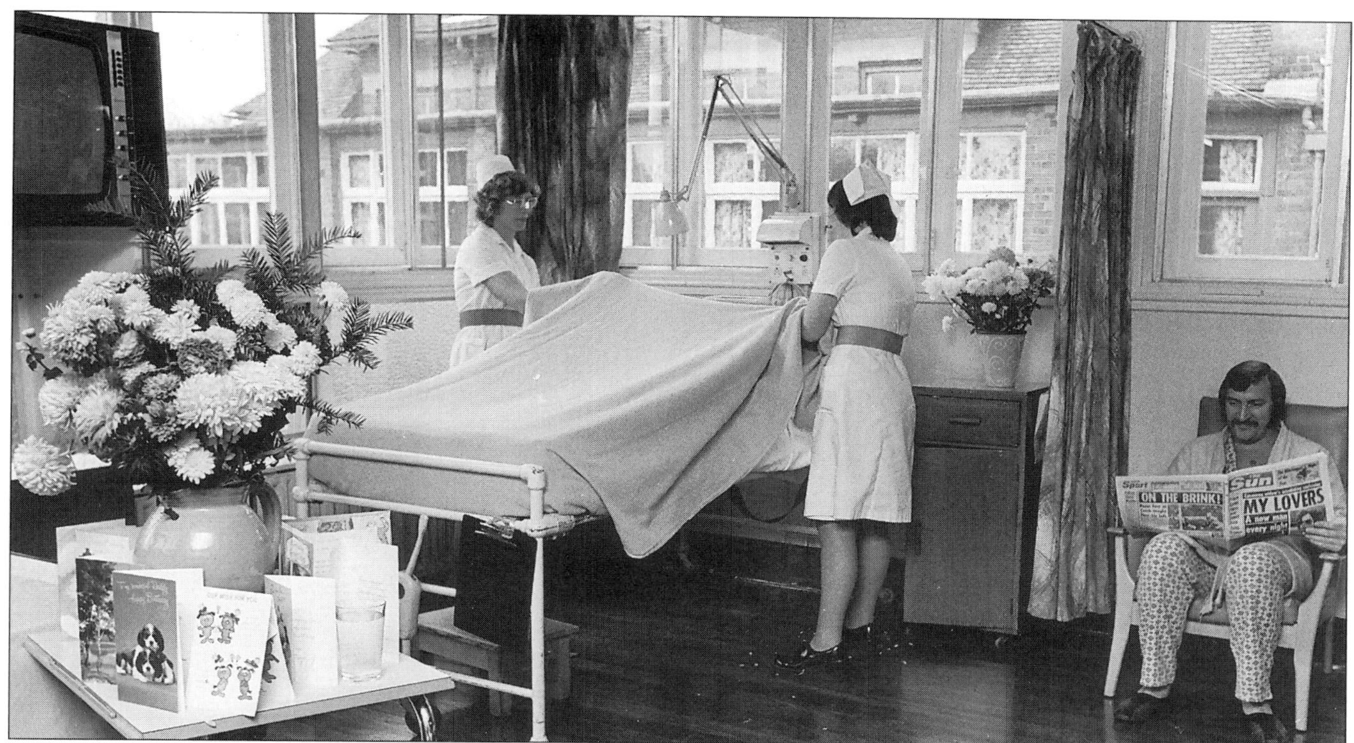

On 8 November 1975 Hinckley Hospital reached its 75th anniversary without fuss or celebration. Instead the work of caring for the sick went on quietly and efficiently. The hospital was formally opened in November 1900 by Mrs C.H.Aldridge of Sketchley. Mr Andrew Jeffcote of Hinckley was the contractor and Mr John Wigg the architect. The *Hinckley Times* reported: 'Once the laying out of the grounds is completed Hinckley will possess a hospital ample for the requirements of the town and district.'

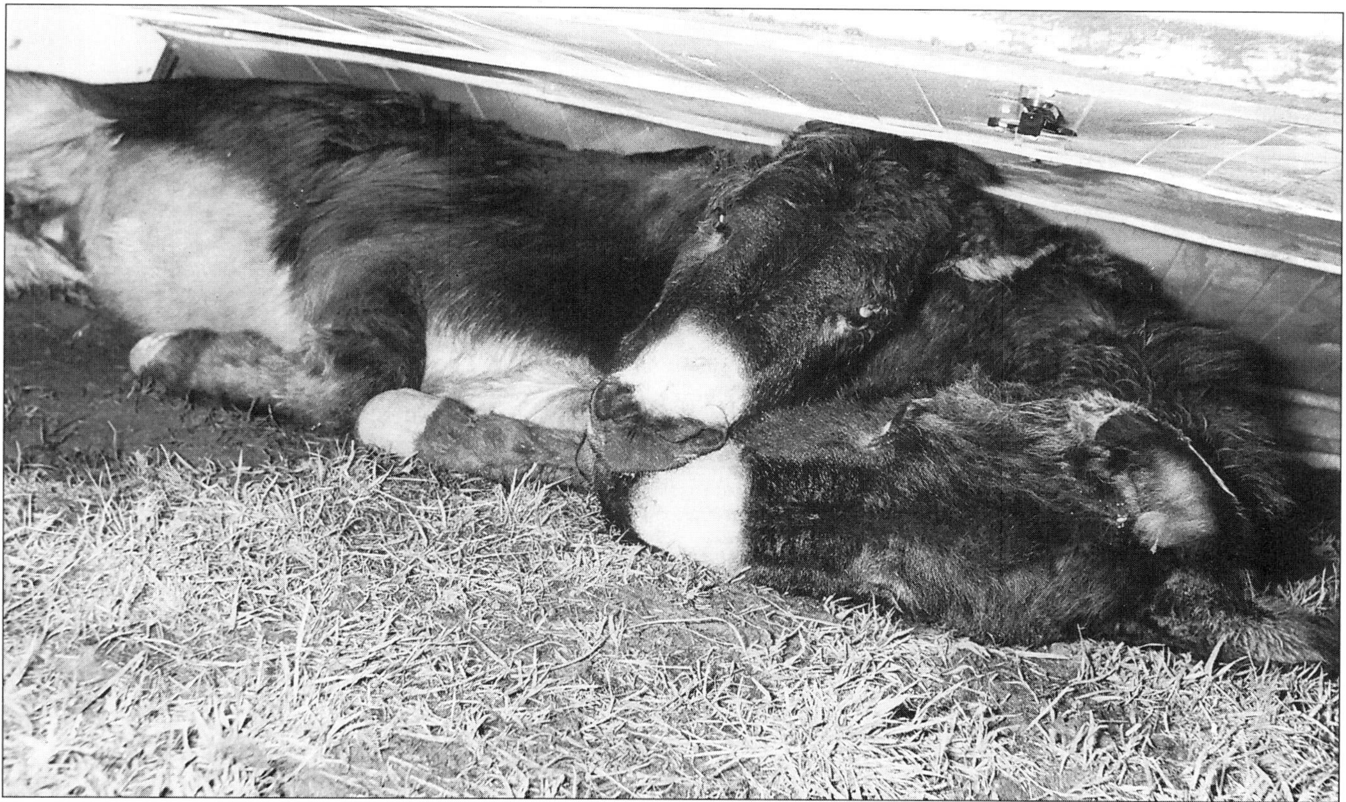

Only Herbie now... Herbie and Jenny were inseparable. The two donkeys owned by Mr Philip Hall of Dadlington lay trapped all night on 9 January 1976 after gales overturned a caravan where they were sheltering. After the caravan was lifted the following morning, Jenny was found dead; Herbie was gently licking her and couldn't understand why she was not following him as usual. It was a sight to moisten the eye of even the most hardened individual.

In July 1976 a huge steel skeleton sprang up on the corner of Trinity Lane and Coventry Road. Hinckley's £1.25 million leisure centre was becoming a reality.

On 30 July 1976 one of Hinckley's most familiar landmarks was felled when the elm which stood on the corner of Spa Lane and London Road became a victim of Dutch Elm Disease.

11 March 1977: 'Blue Skies Over Hinckley For the Visit of Conservative Leader.' reported the *Hinckley Times*. Margaret Thatcher was on a walkabout in the town.

On 1 April 1977 the Trinity Dyeworks at Ashby Road, Hinckley, celebrated its golden jubilee. Pictured here (from left to right) are Mr Len Wilbur (works director), Mr Chris Beal (foreman), Mr Don Pither (executive director), Mr Alf Ballard and Mr Tony Wilbur (foreman). The dyeworks were later demolished and retirement homes were built there and named Ashby Court.

The end of an era on 6 May 1977 as the Joseph Watson Studios on Station Road, Hinckley, closes down. Clearing up, sorting out and settling down for a few quiet moments of reflection is Mr Ernest John Farnell, who ran the shop from 1932 until its demise.

One of the many street parties to celebrate Her Majesty The Queen's Silver Jubilee in June 1977. This one at Bute Close, Holly Croft, Hinckley was obviously enjoyed by all.

On 15 July 1977, the 25km M69 Leicester-Coventry motorway was opened by Mr John Horam, Under Secretary of State for Transport. The new road cost £34 million and it was hoped that it would take most of the traffic off the A46.

In July 1977 the Duke of Edinburgh visited TI Desford Tubes Ltd. Our picture shows a light-hearted moment during the duke's tour of the works. On the right is Mr F.J.England, the managing director of the company.

Marching through Hinckley in July 1977 is the Regimental Band of the 1st Battalion of the Royal Anglian Regiment. The visit to Hinckley came on the second day of their tour of the county.

In November 1977 Trinity Motors staged its first motor show at Hinckley Leisure Centre.

Elizabeth Rathbone (aged ten) and Dawn Slattery (four) try out Hinckley's first 'Pelican Crossing' in October 1977. Borough Council officials were in attendance to explain the system to local people and guide the first users over Ashby Road.

Hinckley Athletic FC's team of October 1977. Back row (left to right): Stuart Martin (trainer), Dick Rushall, Warren Lewis, Mick Taylor, Mick Martin, Ramsay Wilson, Roy Weston, Alan Wykes and Doug Chandler (manager). Front row: Robin Rogers, Tony Canning, Bill Moore, Steve Childs and Terry Taylor.

In November 1977, sappers of the 34th Field Division, Royal Engineers, came to Hinckley's rescue when the regular fire brigade went on strike. In this photograph the makeshift firemen are seen operating a stand-pump with their wartime 'Green Goddess' fire-engine in the background.

His very own road! In November 1977, Mr George Wilkinson of 2 Wortley Cottages, Elmesthorpe is seen standing proudly by the road sign which was about to be changed to Wilkinson Lane to mark his 39 years tending the gardens and graveyard at the Church of St Mary the Virgin, which can be seen in the background.

The Earl Shilton Pantomime Company appeared in January 1978 under its new name, The Theatre Pantomime Company. The name may have changed but the reputation for superb family entertainment remains the same. The 1978 pantomime was *Sleeping Beauty* presented by Jack Marvin and written and produced by Brian Geary. This picture shows Paul Gardner as 'Fetch' and Joan Walker as 'Carry'.

In May 1978 Barwell Treats had its own Princess. Helen Jolly (centre) is seen here with her attendants, from left to right: Joanne Simpson, Louise Bailey, Vicki Ann Conway, Kim Evans, Sophie Brindley and Joanne Holder.

Thousands of spectators lined the route of Hinckley Carnival in June 1978 to watch over 40 tableaux pass by in glorious sunshine. Hinckley's Carnival Queen, Cheryl Cutts, looked resplendent as did her maids, from left to right: Christina Pratt, Margaret Counihan and Joanne Baker.

July 1978: Miss I.C.Furniss up on 'Village Green' at Market Bosworth's 11th Annual Horse Show.

It took Mr Arthur Tomlin three years to build this gate, pictured here in July 1978, based on the Queen's Silver Jubilee. His welding skills were exhibited at the Royal Show and the gate, that weighed in at 3½ cwt was illuminated during the dark hours of winter by what else but a wrought-iron lamp at the entrance to his farm – Wykin House Farm.

Market Bosworth Young Farmers putting their all into the tug o'war at the Annual Horse Show in July 1978.

September 1978: the Premier Works, formerly Toon's on Wood Street, Earl Shilton, already empty for many years, fell victim to a fire that was to render the building dangerous and hasten its demolition. The clock, erected by Mr Alfred Toon, after World War One, was saved due to the efforts of villagers and Mr Denis Brown and it was resited.

October 1978: the 21st John Player Race of the Year at Mallory Park. Kenny Roberts (2) and Tom Heron (27) lead the pack into Gerards, but Barry Sheene went on to win the race.

In October 1978, 33 standard bearers from all over the country attended the Barwell branch of the Royal British Legion's dedication of their new standard.

Actor Tom Baker, television timelord *Doctor Who* in the popular science fiction series, was in Hinckley to autograph copies of the *Doctor Who* books in December 1978. He is seen here with Samuel Newton.

Castle Street, Hinckley, on 26 January 1979 as the heaviest snow for many years fell on the town.

Gloom, doom and misery for Hinckley motorists in January 1979 as empty petrol tanks are the result of another industrial crisis.

In February 1979 the *Hinckley Times* reported: 'Civic Society Fight To Save A Piece Of Old Hinckley'. However, half of King Street was demolished and later rebuilt.

On 9 February 1979, these cottages in Station Road, Stoney Stanton, were among many properties affected when floods hit the Hinckley area.

A pastoral setting of rural peace on a spring morning in March 1979 at Bosworth Park, Market Bosworth.

Nanette Goodman and Chris Clarke as Pierre and Lucy in the Concordia Theatre's production of *Bless the Bride* in May 1979.

Punk rock in the seventies, demonstrated by members of Thurlaston Youth Club at their village's carnival in June 1979.

The Earl Shilton Carnival Princess, Tracey Garner (centre) in June 1979 with her attendants, from left to right: Francesca Hall, Michelle Poxon, Sonja Dominic, Shona Gault, Nicola Lloyd and Suzanne Bailey.

The sun shone on Burbage Carnival in July 1979 and its princesses who led the procession in an open-topped Rolls Royce. They are, left to right: Julie Jenkins, Lucy Cross and Claire Hopkins.

On 8 June 1979, fire destroyed the Unit Sales DIY store at New Buildings, Hinckley.

In June 1979, Mallory Park said farewell to one of the greatest names in motor cycle racing. Fresh from his 14th win on the Isle of Man, 'Mike the Bike' was out of luck when brake failure forced him to retire.

The Goodyear airship flew over Hinckley in July 1979 with a *Hinckley Times* cameraman on board. In this view Derby Road can be seen in the foreground. To the top left Holly Croft Park and its bandstand can be seen.

In this view from the Goodyear airship are the Council offices (top left), Hinckley Health Centre (centre) and Hill Street (bottom right). The houses on the left of Hill Street have been demolished and doctors' surgeries and a pharmacy now stand there.

To a fanfare from the trumpets and drums of the band of the Hinckley Hussars, Hinckley Athletic FC kicked off their centenary season (1979-80) with a 2-0 win over Enderby. Four days later they were soundly beaten 5-2 by a strong Leicester City side. The squad that played against Leicester City were, back row (left to right): Dave Callow (manager), Robin Rogers, Duncan Cooper, Courtney Jones, Derek Jones, Warren Lewis, Mick Martin. Front row: Steve Dean, Terry Taylor, Mick Taylor, Dave Wright, Steve Childs, Mark Stevens, Andy Clark, Stewart Martin (trainer).

At Hinckley Steam Display, Aston Lane, Burbage in September 1979, miniatures line up with their big brothers. A reminder of a bygone age with their ear-piercing whistles and that evocative smell of steam.

A large crowd gathered at Hinckley war memorial in November 1979 for the Remembrance Day service. Silence descended as the standards were lowered in memory of those who lost their lives.

This nativity scene, familiar at schools throughout the Hinckley area, was enacted by children at the St Peter's Roman Catholic School in Earl Shilton in December 1979. Shown here are Clare Farmer and Mark Colden, both aged six, as Mary and Joseph and four-year-olds Zoe Chamberlain and Zoe Bonser as angels.